PRATIBIMBAM (THE REFLECTION)

Sanjoy Kumar Paira

BookLeaf
Publishing

India | USA | UK

Presentation by *BookLeaf Publishing*

Web: www.bookleafpub.com

E-mail: info@bookleafpub.com

ISBN: 9789363312715

First edition 2024

*To my son SAMARJEET (ADI), who fills my
heart with joy each and every day*

ACKNOWLEDGEMENT

There are plenty of people who helped bring this book to fruition, and I am grateful to all of them. Once this book started to go from a concept in my head to a manuscript, there were many people involved who deserve to be acknowledged and thanked– Dr. Arup Kumar Das, Rajib Nandi, Debabrata Ray, Anukul Pradhan, Asanta Bhunia, Chakrapani Das Mahapatra, Aurobindo Das, Sunil Giri, Surja Nandi, Sandip Kumar Maity, Biswasidhu Dey, my parents, and my brothers. Their ideas and suggestions helped me get to a manuscript that made me say, "Yes, it's finally a book!" These people made this book eminently readable. A special thanks to all my friends and students. Most of all, I want to thank my wife and soulmate– GITA DAS PAIRA, for her incredible heart and, as in all things, her unbelievable support. My labour will be amply rewarded if it helps those for whom it is intended. Thanks to all my readers; without you, I would not be here now, writing these words. Especially, I would like to express my humble gratitude to the amazing team at *Book Leaf Publishing* for the help they have rendered in bringing out this book.

PREFACE

"Fill your paper with the breathings of your heart "------William Wordsworth

The reflective poetry of poet and artist Sanjay Paira enthralled me in countless ways. Simple, yet profound, impressive dealing with the facts and figures of nature, affection, and mundaneness of everyday life captivated my heart. In most of the places, I have found that there is tremendous creative usage of words, rhythms, and intonation. Sanjay's poetry is evocative, smelling of rains and parched soils, speaking of self-respect from ancient scriptures, and tottering to the finer moments spent in a nature story. His artistic sense enchants all of his poetry.

This collection of poems, PRATIBIMBAM ('The Reflection'), I am sure will go a long way in cementing the emotional bond among the readers since these poems share a lot of common concerns, anxieties, hopes, attitudes and visions of the present and future.

Sometimes, it seems that his verses are in obscurity. These are full of symbolism and occultism. One must have ample knowledge to understand the sound of his poems and thoughts. These poems will be immensely useful and joyful to hundreds of readers.

The theme of a poem is always its central topic, subject, or message. Sanjay begins his poem 'The Death of Spring' by talking about nature, seasons, and flowers and how they are calm and quiet. He says the same about 'my little cottage filled with the light of their colours' comparing to the 'knocking at the door of my poverty'. The recurring message here is that nothing golden and beautiful lasts. The mood of this poem is one of wonder and exploration. It invokes the marvel of learning new things.

However, here, the mood becomes darker and sinister in 'Spring has died.' The tone of Sanjay's poems is mostly satirical, serious, and critical. But these are appreciative. The use of imagery and sensory language shows the depth and vividness of his work. Some other literary devices, like metaphors, personification, flashbacks, symbolism, and diction, have also been used by Sanjay.

Sanjay's grammar can seem daunting, but it's just a matter of breaking it down.

Capitalization of whole word, use of Present Perfect instead of Past – really commendable. His capitalization of 'THEY' in 'Neophobia' is in order to emphasize the main focus of the poetry.

Uses of metaphorical phrases, like 'swallowing the dry facts', 'everyone's Yamuna and Indus' and 'the eyes of knowledge' in the poem 'Education', 'knocking at the door of my poverty', 'fierce paws of winter' and 'the sky of love' in 'Death of Spring', 'poisonous breath of the invisible yet powerful serpent' and 'tongues of mythical, monstrous dragons' in 'Neophbia', 'totalitarian paw' and 'hellish door' in 'Green Friends', 'Aromatic food' in 'Hunger' easily conquer the hearts of the readers. The other notable grammatical element in Sanjay's poem is the abundance of Ellipses. Almost every line of 'Neophobia' ends in an Ellipsis (......) to signify the continuation, suspense, and omission in the context. The rhythm and structure of Sanjay's poetry are also unique. Sometimes we see rhyme, sometimes free verse, sometimes blank verse, and sometimes a narrative one. With regard to 'Green Friends', this poem belongs to the genre of free verse and depicts the social issues that existed at the time of its creation. With reference to the poem's imagery, the devices present mostly appeal to the reader's visual and tactile senses. It uses a pastoral setting and appeal to evoke an idealized image of rural life in the reader's mind. Obviously, nature, in the eyes of Sanjay, has much more romance in it than any kind of leisure activity most modern city inhabitants would prefer when he says, 'Their love for us will never be ended'. I would say that Sanjay's poetry is filled with emotion and inspiration. He employs a wide usage of metaphors, similes, personifications, and other poetic devices, which make his works colourful and engaging. The choice of words is exacting, and he has done justice to the connotations and denotations of them. Most of the line-breaking seems natural, almost as if the lines have been written spontaneously in a surge of inspiration. However, with the conciseness and effectiveness of the language, his devotion to poetic work is really praiseworthy. I feel very fortunate to have the opportunity to write a preface on behalf of 'The Reflection'. I offer my heartfelt love to Sanjay. Let us think of our differences and get united through the everlasting human bond that Sanjay's poetry can create and believe that the future belongs as much as our lives– 'the soul of nature'.

Best wishes
Debabrata Roy
Director,
ALAPAN

(Academy for Language Advancement &
Progressive Attitude Nurturing)

THE SHADOW

I am today fatigued, restless and frenzied
I don't know what to do
I am slowly fading away
A hideous black shadow is following me.
My whole body is trying to possess my mind
with its ugly paws.
I want to be freed..... freed.
No..... there is no escape from his grasp.
It is impossible to escape from his merciless
gaze
He is always my companion, day and night..
everywhere
I can't tolerate him anymore
Again...
I can't live without him
In the light of day, he is gradually becoming
monstrous
That body is huge, curvy...
His hunger is boundless
Who wants to tear me to pieces by using his
hairy body as a weapon
My body and mind are tired today
Oh God!
A ray of hope...

The only way to escape from his ferocious clutches...
My death!
yes.. yes.. my death
My death is my freedom!
But will he release me?
Maybe not...
Maybe... My worn-out body will be stuck in the ashes forever
Because...
He is my reflection

FREEDOM

By selling values, humanity and conscience in the market, freed from the glory of self-glorification, some lowly vermin spread the message of freedom by dressing themselves in the lantern of patriotism.

However........
Freedom is still not free
 All day long, avoiding the gaze of some greedy eyes,
A Rose growing on the sidewalk, looking hopelessly at the empty dish and... asking for freedom.
 Just two pieces of freedom

In the scorching sun, Even the sleepy border
guard with sleepy eyes looks at the way back
home,
 And wants freedom.
The grown-ups are looking for freedom today in
the light-dark stream of modernity.
 Tired of bearing the burden of rusted education,
the head of the future wants freedom today.
 Caught in the complex web of planetary stars,
the newborn seeks freedom to breathe.
But freedom is still not free.

HUNGER

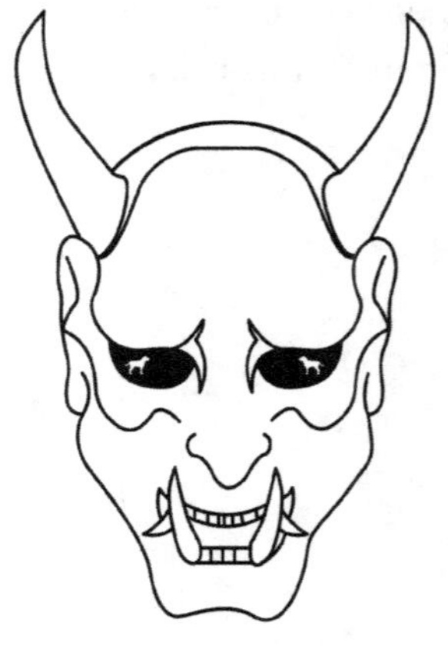

Hundreds of dishes filled with aromatic food
were lying on the side of the road,
 A little beggar's daughter comes running
happily.
 So many types of food piles
What a great smell!
 With a mouth full of hunger, she runs to get his
share of the food,
 A kennel of dogs came running to nab those.
Started barking, Screaming and fighting
 After licking the food,
 They went away
 The hungry girl gazes at the empty dishes with
her hopeless eyes
 covering the mouth with hands

She cried out deeply...
Good Heavens!
Why we're deprived of everything – It is useless
to live in vain in this world.

EDU-CIRCUS

The spines of the future are worn and faded
today, carrying the burden of knowledge like a
mountain.
 The bright dreams of the future are slowly
suffocating them
 They are desperate and eager to get some fresh,
free air
 They strive to erect towers of hope with bent
spines
 The fresh saplings are today dull and lifeless by
killing their own desires with the wreath of
hopes, desires, frowns, neglect and indifference.
 Today they spend many sleepless nights while
fulfilling the dreams of others
 They look at the sky with emotionless eyes and
count the days waiting for just a piece of the star.
 Burned by the fire of directionless education,
tender childhoods have lost their light
 It was supposed to be the sun they were trying
to burn like the flickering flame of a candle
today
 With a little love, they too can become the sun.
 Can bloom
 Being a colourful green tree, can provide cool
shade to others

Can dream of a happy world
Can sing the song of victory
In the upcoming future, they can be the walking
sticks of their parents
can be the foundation of the future
Can build a universe without violence and
hunger.

NATURE–THE GREATEST TEACHER

Being exhausted, I took rest under a banyan tree
on the side of a deserted road.

Ah! What a cool shade, what immense peace,
the mind was filled with bliss.

I saw and learned a lot!

Which built a bridge of endless joy between
my heart and empty soul.

The branches of old banyan tree touching the
ground taught–

Life has to be close to the ground

With a sound of patterning, the ripe fruits of the
banyan tree fall freely on the ground taught–

One day, everyone has to leave after attaining
the fullness of life.

The tender leaves swaying in the gentle breeze taught–
The pace of life never stops.
The banyan tree and the peepal tree that grew entwined taught us to grow up together rather than competing.
 the buzzing flies attracted by the smell of ripe fruits taught–
Never neglect duty, no matter how small or big.
The dry, lifeless bark of the tree taught me to think–
Appearance and youthfulness are transient, lived through action.
The blowing gentle breeze taught–No more rest, Friend.
Miles to go before I sleep.
With a mystical touch of nature, both my feet touched the ground of reality.
I understood the real truth of life.
The pace of life never stops.
Life continues to flow in its own rhythm forever.
Nature is the heart of life, which is spontaneous, fresh, green and vibrant.
Life does not exist in iron, stone, or brick.
Nature is the source of the creation of life.
Therein lies the secret of life and happiness.
Realization can only be achieved by stepping out of the shell of busyness.

MOTHER

Mother is the first word of affection expressed by a child
 Mother is the first love of a child's life. Mother is a pure divine face
 A mother is a boundless ocean of selfless love
 A mother is a stream of love amid strict discipline
 Mother means the goddess of love and compassion
 A mother is a simple solution to a hundred obstacles
 Mother means to hold the child in pain
 Mother means strengthening the fear of the world by relying on the worn-out backbone

Mother means dressing the burn wound with agony

A mother is the hand that wipes the child's tears from her tear-soaked eyes.

A mother is a beautiful face that endures a hundred sorrows and indifferences and wishes the child well with a smile

A mother is a ray of hope in the darkness of despair

Mother means a lamp that burns itself and illuminates others

Mother is a divine image of God

One of the most beautiful gifts to give to a child is a mother made with the soil of love and affection.

EDUCATION

Education is not just about swallowing the dry facts.
Education means enlightening the lamp of knowledge in the core of the mind
Education means controlling your emotions and then trying to react
Education does not mean you are Muslim and I am Hindu.
Education means establishing communal harmony and spreading brotherhood
Education means Ganga is everyone's Yamuna or Indus.
Education means letting caste differences be removed from the mind.
Education means destroying superstitions in the light of reform.
Education means being polite, humble, good, and kind
Education means letting the inferiority complex die completely
Education means seeing a new India through the eyes of knowledge.
Education will unlock the secret of staying lively
Education means protesting against the wall of bigotry.

Education means worshipping the truth, never telling a lie
Education means never giving up, just try and try
Education means forgetting hatred and love for all
Education means through the touch of knowledge purifying your soul
Education means do not forget the motherland where you have taken birth
Education means, through planting trees, saving nature as well as our Earth
Education is a gift that will enlighten your life
Education means stepping ahead, forgetting the pain and strife

NEOPHOBIA

Behind old, torn leaves
   The new bud is in the middle of an oscillation
Subconsciously unbearable fear of stings,
   The mind is tired of inevitable thoughts
   Tenderness of immense beauty is lost to the
deadly and poisonous breath of the invisible yet
powerful serpent
   The passion to absorb the new in the face,
   The courage to achieve new things hangs in the
core of mind today.
   The giant ancient tree is now sapless and
defoliated between the venomous, slitting
tongues of mythical, monstrous dragons.
   Seeing his own reflection in imagination

You can paint a picture of reality by using the
colors of blood
But...
Hardness cannot be overstated
Neglected, miserable, exploited, hated,
oppressed, hungry, the proletariats are still
cheated, deprived.
The stunned world stares apprehensively.....
The reluctance to orbit the sun is obvious,
but-----
The rules are very strict.
day by day...
Its hardness also surpasses power
THEY are helpless...
Who makes the key to breaking the rules even
today?

A FLAME

A unique hero was born in a farmer's house
with a pair of gleaming eyes, a raised head.
His feet swing in rhythm,
his chest is adorned with love
He is a Human form of Nataraja, engrossed in
dance.
The goddess Saraswati lives in his voice
The light of Trinetra (third eye) is always
spreading the energy of his soul
His body language is intense, like the smile on
his face
He is a dreamer.
Humility is his word, love is his language
He burns despair and always awakens hope.
With the blessings of parents, his body is
nourished
He is Submissive to Guru, excellent in character.
He slaves Criticism of society, frowns, hatred,
insults
And....
Make them clap their hands under his feet.
Pain is his friend; sorrow is his companion
People's love is always his companion.
Like a king or a warrior, he is never afraid of
anything

None can extinguish the fire of his rage
Softness within him is like soil, he is the
embodiment of strong humanity,
No matter how much you (society) talk about
him
God is always with him, like a shadow
So, love him
If you want to get love from him
Remove the veil of darkness of your mind, you
will see the light
Love is the panacea of all diseases like
ignorance, indifference and hatred
Love deeply to tie an eternal knot with him
Hence...
Spread love to make our Earth smile

GREEN FRIENDS

They, our best friends, the soul of nature,
 So kind, so beautiful, entrancing like our
Mother.
 Adore us like babies,
Lay down their lives over and over
Spreading their shade of love,
 Shedding their Green Blood
 Always protect us from rain, sun and flooding.
They think us friends but we don't think them so,
 we tear them up with our totalitarian paw.
Their love for us will never be ended,
 Their endearment for us is above and beyond.

our selfishness, covetousness always snatch their
breath away,
They are panting, losing their breathing, turning
out to be pale and rawboned day by day.
To keep our existence on Earth
Love them, plant them more,
Or else----
 The graveyard is not so far
 The 'Lord of Death' is knocking at the hellish
door.
They are our saviour
Care them, save them for future
 Or else----
 The Earth will be altered into a sterile desert ,
The day is not so far.

A MAN WITH A GOLDEN HEART

When my mind was restless
And full of sadness,
You removed my solitude
And filled it with happiness.
When losing my colour
I was in the dark,
You lightened it
With your positive spark.
When I was exhausted....
And just fighting with my negativity,
You taught me how to deal with positivity.
When I was captivated by the spell of illusion,
With your magic wand, you gave me the
solution.

When I was repulsed and everything was going
out of my way,
Then you turned up like a saviour....
And taught me the mantras to be gay.
I always looked upon you as my inspiration
Because you made a path for me...
To share my twisted thoughts, feelings and
emotions.
You're irrevocable, festal, polite and jubilant,
You're a man with a golden heart, a beautiful
mind and valiant.
You have an infectious smile
And you're pure at heart,
Which teaches me to love others rather than
hurt.

FRAGRANCE

As soon as I lost my sense of wonder, I realized
I was terribly trapped in a spider's web
 Eight bloody eyes and legs bent on wounding
me
 I screamed…
 but
 The sound was lost in an echoless void
 Then...
 Then the sound of his cheer sent a wave of fear
through my entire body
 I woke up with a hypnotised, bruised body.
 My past, present and future are fading before
my eyes
 My consciousness is disappearing into space

I came back to reality again under the pull of
gravity
   The harshness, dryness, are more terrible than
the colourful imagination of the unknown,
dreamy world.
   I suddenly regained consciousness.
 In the overwhelming fragrance of jasmine
flowers, I saw myself standing with bare feet
underneath a dilapidated, dry peepul
A bunch of jasmine flowers is in my hand.

DEATH OF SPRING

On a calm, sunny afternoon, a gloomy, cold
winter wind came knocking at the door of my
poverty.
  I quietly opened the door and found a bunch of
gulmohar lying on my doorstep.
  My little cottage was filled with the light of
their colours
  In the fierce paws of winter, the dry and faded
cottage of mine regained new life
  I watched in amazement
   In the distance...
  A little lass is standing under a gulmohar tree
  Her black body is flowing with the sound of
new youth.

A drowsy depth in her black eyes stares blankly
at me,
 the tenderness, brightness of spring gave the
form of the lass with rainbow colours.
 The lass is waiting for me under the sky of
love...
 Suddenly, with a scream, the lass disappeared
in a gust of wind
 again...
 A very cold gust of wind twisted all my
thoughts
 Far away, a desperate cuckoo cried out.
 The wind came to me and whispered, 'Spring
has died'.

THE MIRAGE

I am madly in love with you at first sight.
  Yes – you are the one for whom I have crossed
from the wild Africa to the hot desert of
Rajasthan.
  I looked at you with lustful eyes.
 Oh! how beautiful you are---
  The brightness of the sun, the softness of the
moon have shaped you.
 You are spring!
  You are a living canvas in nature's mirror.
I tried to catch you like a weary, thirsty traveller
--
But alas!
You are a mirage!
 My mind, soul are obsessed with you.

I tried to get rid of--
 But, I am trapped under the spell of your
rose-blooded lips.
 You are a dreamer!
 You flow like a river in my veins.
 I am willing to follow your orbit forever.
 I just want to hug you with both my hands...
 But alas!
 Your body is disappearing into a gloomy grey
fog.
 Ignoring a gust of cold wind, I ran like a
madman --
 All I got was a handful of utter darkness

THE OMNIPOTENT

You may be very strong
  You may be the richest and happiest person in
this Universe
But....
  You are no greater than DEATH
 All are equal to Death
 The same weight for all on the scale of death,
maybe you are at the highest peak of the law
  but......
  In the eyes of the law of death, you are
ordinary, insignificant, like others.
  Death is true, death is beautiful, death is the
only way to be freed
  Death ignores no one.

Death hates no one.
Death does not see success.
Death does not see money.
Death does not see how rich, how poor you are.
Death is very generous
He invites Everyone.
Everything, except death, is worthless.
So let's just say it in a loud voice--
I will wear the garland of death with my love

LOVE IS INVINCIBLE

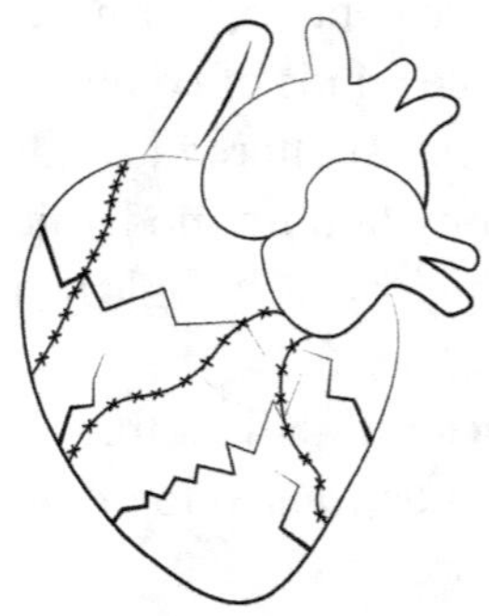

Does LOVE die?
  Or – the spirit of love is still incorruptible,
imperishable, immortal.
  The mystery of love is still in different forms of
exploitation, oppression, cruelty and brutality.
  The slits of the black serpent purify the soul
encased in the foetid skin of the venomous
creature.
Behind the imperishable soul's rough, loveless
living shell
  The hornets are still today
 Who indulges in the glittering knives and tastes
the blood of the angel of love.
  Also--

Society grits its teeth in front of the dirty square box and changes the channel to the empathy button

God's instrument of punishment is today enslaving the winds of commerce.

The classically cultured love of the bitterness of the monotony of ultra-modernity is unable to express the glory of self-glory in the irony of pomp.

To get back the selfless freedom even today

Two new buds wanted to grow in the soft rays of loving caress

Petals had the unrestrained unrest to touch the aliveness

Falling sun was the diary of dream choice.

All that was left was the touch of love's spiritual writing.

In the labyrinth called God's life, it is incomplete, unfinished.

God's idiosyncrasy may have been in the name of establishing love, just like establishing the religion of war in the Mahabharata

Two soft, green hearts were wound in the morgue

What is the cruelty of God!

Is it in the name of relieving the disease in love medicine but getting the God of two tender hearts? Or by freeing society from the clutches of commercial love

New buds of love's inspirational Mantra for
Blossoming.
William Blake's sickly rose's beautiful petals
Even today some barbarous insects decapitate
the soul of love and enjoy their cruelty.
The stupid box still encourages them to show
how weak and helpless this old society is?
 But one day...
  By untying the irony, ringing the bell of
punishment,
 The righteous mother's black-ribbed barrier,
with tears streaming down her eyes,
 Unburdens the yoke of iniquity with the scale of
justice,
 break the chains of injustice,
  The black-clad society will sing the song of
love,
 Freed from the dungeon of caste and religion,
the mind of the new generation
  The lines of dilemma–spontaneous questioning
will fade little by little--
 - Does LOVE die?

WINGS OF HOPE

In the midst of extreme busyness, the baby of the mind is largely neglected today.

The baby that grows in the nest of peace is disappearing.

The jewel of the mind is only immense passion, curiosity and inquisitiveness

Unlimited curiosity to know the unknown

There is no time for anxiety, depression, worry about the future

Today, we ourselves are the ultimate losers in trying to conquer time.

Today the bird of mind is unable to fly despite having two wings

The two wings are now burdened with responsibility

A strong desire to fly in the face but the legs are bound by its chains

A deafening cry is coming from the heart of the
mind
  I want to live
 Live–let me live too
  But when it came to the mouth, it disappeared
in a gust of wind
  The baby of mind growing behind the dry skin
of old age is slowly growing old
  The faded feathers of freedom's wings are
falling little by little
  Determined to fly in the free, calm sky
whenever he gets the chance
  The baby of the mind must be saved
  Otherwise, it is useless to die without glory.

METAMORPHOSIS

One secluded afternoon, suddenly eyes fell on a
leaf of a peepal tree leaning in the distance
 A hairy, fat and lazy caterpillar
 Resting after lunch.
Being Very angry
 I thought of killing.
 I suppressed my instinct in the hope of meeting
some new creation
 He looked at me blankly
 Like, I've known him for a long time--
  "There is no danger from me," he said, shaking
his head from side to side
 Friend, now I am at rest.
 You can go

As soon as I turn my eyes away from the
caterpillar,
 Suddenly...
 The whole world changed before the eyes.
 In no time, I saw my little peepal tree had
turned into an unknown giant prehistoric tree.
 and---
 Little by little, the caterpillar rolled its body
into a huge cocoon.
 then----
 An enormous butterfly slowly broke through
the cocoon.
 What large four wings! How bright and
colourful they are!
 I could clearly hear the sound of his wings.
 I was stunned, speechless and perplexed at the
same time.
 Both my feet were bound to the ground
 I could not move away from there, even with
all my mental strength.
 Mesmerized, I saw red, yellow, green, purple
colours falling from its wings.
 And......
 They fall to the ground, creating innumerable
butterflies.
 My surprise was suddenly broken by my
mother's call.

I came back to the real world again and was
surprised to see the deserted afternoon as if it
were evening.
But where is that tree?
Not even that caterpillar
I stand alone in a void.
Very alone
Very alone.

WOUNDS OF LOVE

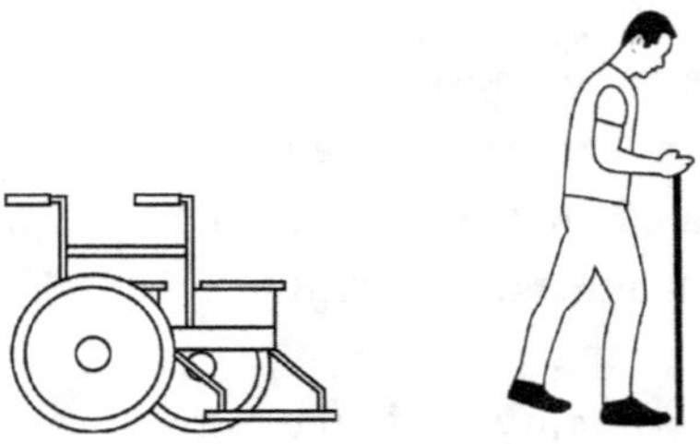

I heard that men don't cry
  But I saw my father crying.
 every time...
 That cry is soundless, so deep yet deafeningly
emotional, tearless and as mysterious as the
lonely sea.
  Yes, because of me.
  I am the one---
 Who repeatedly hurt his love's ribs.
 The man wanted to bind everyone in the vine
of love
  But...
 I am a fruitless flower.
 Whose beautiful, dreamy past lives today with
an uncertain present and future. Father's

affection is weightless today on the scale of
love.
 I wanted to cry--
  But I couldn't.
  I am the father, how to cry?
  The boundless ocean of anger, hatred,
accumulated on itself in every nerve of memory
says again and again in regret--
  Men don't cry.
 I don't look at myself in the mirror.
  Behind a bush of thick beard and moustache
that devilish, irresponsible face frowned again
and again–
 Don't forget you too, Dad.
  The past will repeat itself.

SUFFERING OF CREATION

It is impossible to create only with colour and brush
  Creation cannot occur without the awakening
of the artistic being.
 To create,
 Must have a creative, artistic mind.
  Happy people, satisfied people cannot be artists
 An artist sacrifices all the achievements of life.
  A person living a luxurious life can never fulfil
his desire to be an artist.
leave the shell of comfort
stand on the rough ground and witness the
reality
 Pictures can be painted in the colours of
imagination
 But...

Reality cannot be overstated.
An artist's life is never comfortable.
A true artist turns away from comfort
A true artist is engrossed in sensual pain.
because......
If there is no suffering, there is no creation
A sorrowful mind is a reference point for
creativity
A true artist has to protest against neglect,
hatred, immense sorrow and portray the harsh
and cruel form of society in the colours of
heartbroken blood, sweat and tears.
History is a witness
Many artists have had to face death with a
smile in the name of protest.
This society does not respect a true artist. Does
not give real dignity
Not worth his time
Laughs about his art-being
Wants to buy his creation
but ....
Artist cannot be bought
An artist is nobody's slave
A true artist is a priceless asset
He cannot be bought
He cannot be bought

PURSUIT OF HAPPINESS

Happiness, sadness, suffering, pain are the four
hands of the clock of life,
 Its discordant, rhythmic ups and downs Send
life deep into the bottomless valley.
 Petals of happiness can be torn to pieces by
ferocious caterpillars in an instant.
What a great fool is the Man!
 Although he thinks himself to be the lord of all
riches,
 is still beyond the power of man to buy
happiness,
 The slave of sorrow...
 Attempts to catch it are ongoing.
 But....
 Utter failure
 These fools who are constantly chasing money
do not know that money is also the slave of
happiness
 The creatures (human) who seek the existence
of happiness in the big things are today making
the tiny pleasures very alone.
 They can also be friends if we extend our
hands.
 Money cannot buy happiness, and nobody
wants to buy sorrow.

Man is the infinite creation of the Supreme God

Despite being so advanced in science and technology, we failed to make instruments to make ourselves happy

In fact, the endless pursuit of catching the sun has turned man into a ridiculously strange creature.

www.ingramcontent.com/pod-product-compliance
Lightning Source LLC
LaVergne TN
LVHW021250200726
843509LV00012B/1627